BROADLANDS

'Some creatures in *Broadlands* most likely have never been taken into poetry before. Little local lives are here everywhere present – lives knelt to and felt under fingertips – the eggs of a wren hidden in a leaf-dome nest in a bramble tangle. Matt Howard's way of seeing, and his plain and yet charged writing of his attentiveness, yields poems that are proof – the finest I've seen recently – that poets might be the best nature-writers of our times. Matt Howard's poems know that nature's own writing – how a wren lives, say – will never be the same as our writing of nature. The wonder-soaked seeing and lovable cautious modesty of this collection is highly intelligent as to the gap between nature and nature-writing, but its poems make that same gap narrower than it is in almost any other comparable contemporary book.' – TIM DEE

Matt Howard was born in Norfolk in 1978. He is a poet and environmentalist who worked in various roles for the RSPB for more than a decade.

His first pamphlet *The Organ Box* was published by Eyewear in 2014. His debut collection *Gall* was published by *The Rialto* in 2018, and his second book-length collection, *Broadlands*, by Bloodaxe in 2024. *Gall* won the inaugural Laurel Prize for Best First Collection in 2020 and the 2018 East Anglian Book Award for Poetry and was also shortlisted for the 2019 Seamus Heaney Centre First Collection Prize.

Matt is also an editor and events programmer. He co-founded the RSPB and *The Rialto* Nature and Place Poetry Competition in 2011 and was co-editor of *Magma 72 – The Climate Change Issue*. He has served as a trustee and steering group member of New Networks for Nature, an eco-organisation comprising a broad alliance of creators working to assert the central importance of landscape and nature in our cultural life. He has been poet in residence for the Cambridge Conservation Initiative and also the Wordsworth Trust. Since 2018 he has been a trustee of *The Rialto*, and was Douglas Caster Cultural Fellow in Poetry at the University of Leeds 2021-2023.

His website is: https://linesofmigration.co.uk/

MATT HOWARD

Broadlands

BLOODAXE BOOKS

ISBN: 978 1 78037 688 2

First published 2024 by
Bloodaxe Books Ltd,
Eastburn,
South Park,
Hexham,
Northumberland NE46 1BS.

www.bloodaxebooks.com
For further information about Bloodaxe titles
please visit our website and join our mailing list
or write to the above address for a catalogue.

Supported using public funding by
ARTS COUNCIL
ENGLAND

Cover design: Neil Astley & Pamela Robertson-Pearce.

Printed in Great Britain by Bell & Bain Limited, Glasgow, Scotland, on
acid-free paper sourced from mills with FSC chain of custody certification.

ACKNOWLEDGEMENTS

Acknowledgements are due to the editors of the following publications in which a number of these poems previously appeared: *Anthropocene*, *Bad Lilies*, *Channel*, *The Dark Horse*, *Finished Creatures*, *Lighthouse*, *Magma*, *Natural Light*, *New Humanist*, *The New Statesman*, *The North*, *Poetry and Audience*, *Poetry Birmingham Literary Journal*, *The Poets at Dove Cottage: Poems about the Wordsworths and the Lake District* (Smith|Doorstop, 2022), *The Poetry Review*, *The Rialto*, *Spelt*, *Stand*, *Wild Court* and *Write Where We Are Now*.

I owe a debt of gratitude to many who have so generously given their advice and enthusiasm: Matt Haw, Colin Hughes, Michael Mackmin, Esther Morgan, Jos Smith and John Whale.

A further thank you to the following who also helped and supported me: Mark Cocker, John Fanshawe, Nick Stone and Mike Toms. And all the dear friends and colleagues at RSPB past and present, who have contributed in so many ways to the making of this book.

For residencies and assistance, I am grateful to Arts Council England, the Cambridge Conservation Initiative and the Wordsworth Trust.

Especial thanks to Douglas Caster and the University of Leeds for the life-changing gift of a Fellowship.

And above all to Amanda, with my love and gratitude for everything.

CONTENTS

Stand in Late May

Take this manky ditch off the Yare,
this heat-stink of algae blooming –
what with all the ploughing to the margins,

abstraction of water, and run-off
into the marshes, there's such choked chances.
But in and about this scrutty reed,

here at least, a rhizal stand of yellow flag again.
Broadsword stems, forged from the sunk under
blades that splay to these blazing iris tongues,

each with the little zag of their nectar guide.
What's to be done but keep going?
The world is in such increments.

With so much more and more at stake,
I tell you now, for what it's worth,
here's where I hilt my every word.

Reedbed

Out for parasitised reed warbler nests all day
and my eyes stung with that glare off the fen;
then this night, thoughts deserting, through more-than-dream,
my mind flitting those hectares, our room and elsewhere.

I saw that man with hands cupped to his mouth
on the lode bank, the wind at his back,
such mimicry calling the cuckoo in –
where any of this sits with necessity or cruelty.

And now you shift in our nest-cup,
the next day gaping like a nestling cuckoo
as eye to eye we are bleared awake with a look
that says, *regardless, I am here for you.*

Nest Surveying I, 17/4/17

TL 86843 80674

Note it all down. Shadwell Track, bottom wood;
this is concerned with time and known position –
the GPS app gives the coordinates
(from the precision of ground clocks synchronised
with satellites' orbiting planes and atomic clocks).

But still, you have to follow the quick of a wren's mind.
Under a crown of dew-matted bracken, old blood, orange-brown,
a dome of sticks and grass on a bramble crossbeam
with a year-old hawthorn lintel, a couple of weeks into leaf.
Three quarters of a metre above nettles.

And sure she's momentarily off, kneel.
Snake the burr of your left arm, blind, to the entrance,
then inside, place a fingertip on the whelm of each.
Note: four eggs in total, unpredated, cold or just cooling –
which is the beginning of an answer to everything.

Cults of Broadland

Fen raft spider

Let us venerate niche and otherness,
local, patch-level occurrence –
take the fen raft spider's
each simple eye, each leg hair sensing

the water's tension. All his
drawn out care, a display of front legs
in arcs across the meniscus, that moving
slenderness, stop-start, from side to side.

She watches while he grooms.
Now receptive, they bob slowly.
And his front legs flicker,

vibrating all over her abdomen.
She draws herself in so he can roll them
on her back into their rippling.

Fen orchid

There are studies concerned with presence
at the Botanic Garden in Cambridge,
where they harvest the mycorrhizal fungus
essential for germination and growth.

All I understand is as far as I can see –
June to July on a fen in Norfolk,
peaty mud staining my knees,

that yellowy-green, the broad-lip base leaf,
its blend-in with the part-chewed sward,
each little barb off the one soft spike
set on this floating ground.

Milk parsley / swallowtail
7th–11th July 2017

All cults must have their curses:
may this curse of losses befall
the bastard or bastards
who dug out milk parsley at Hickling,
taking with it as many as twenty
or more swallowtail caterpillars.

And may they one day, sometime soon,
find themselves again under the breadth
of a searing blue broadland sky,
in t-shirts and shorts, or better yet, topless
about their work, as the sap and hairs
of giant hogweed catch them,
so that they metamorphose
to a blistered imago,
all the shame bursting their skin.

Queen Wasp

Watch now this absolute
this need and certainty
wakened again to begin
making and making
grubbing one thing
undoing another her
with such linear progress
all scratch and claw
levering the surface
working each grain
each hewn line
the shed door's slats
treated and weathered wood
lifting with the work
of her mouth parts
her grafting rough-planed
and brighter in her wake

while you can get close
see the facets of compound eyes
with head-down focus
now jaws chew and pulp
by her own saliva
knowing to site the nest
inside the shed
going easily through a gap
to the roof ridge underside
shy of light setting about the spindle
the first papery nest strut
moulded by her mouth
now the start of an inverted cup
the growing form of it
malleable as her shuttling
back to her track
and brighter in her wake

watch each day
the sprawl morphing
she'll wall herself in
all her emergent workers come
her emissaries and avarice
how they mould it
all in service
the door sunk on its hinge
the mouth of one secreted to many
kindling the season's heat
swelling each mouth swollen
more pulp more heat
seeping of coal tar from old sleepers
the drone and thrum of her number
her laying more queens more chances
brighter in her wake
carrying such vulgar intonations

See how the rotary ditcher is

making all this, with each pass
the sun jagging off steel, its cutting angles
led by a cyclops laser eye, profiling –

our hauled bulk and radials
gnarling a dream of mud, freshwater,
spuming spoil, excavating great lengths

of foot drains, shallow pools, fresh lymph nodes
off the main dykes. There's a new fringe
already waking in the wing mirrors,

micro topographies of soil, cleft and lifted
marsh falling back as more of itself. This
nowhere-middle of Berney, below sea level,

the fag-end of a heathen summer,
thundering under a slab of Broadland sky.
These muck scars will not last.

Each pass is to pass on. What is and will yet be.
Here's grazing for wigeon and pink-feet
in a matter of weeks, where just a season will yield

tussocks of redshank, lapwing scrapes,
chicks about the midge larvae in new wet edges.
We're no more than tending a body of water

that'll bloom the tumbling displays to come,
spread primaries mirroring in pools,
flashing the sky's own outstretched offerings.

There's all the earth moved. The key turned,
now the heavy-legged comedown from the cab,
back to the hardstanding under your boots.

Fen Meadow

After that wildness of rain, a month's fall
in little more than a day, bless them, the Field Teachers,
for this drenching, with yet another group of early primary kids.

Liberated or herded, they're going in their rough formation,
trudging to the meadow even as it starts up again.
Today there's nothing to conjure for them to see,

no harriers or late dragonflies, no butterflies up in this,
no singing, and any orchids are long since gone under.
That meadow's a month sunken into autumn.

All are in their waterproofs and boots –
that brightness gathering for the lesson
in this wet misery, their joy in the just-being-out.

Now is when they let them know how and why
this ground cuts up under their feet, that here,
we're only floating on all the grown and growing things,

and *by jumping together, we move the whole world.*
Up they go, bewildered and delighted,
almost instantly landing, feeling the ground shift and righting.

Just look at the air about them, the peat spatters,
that earthy freshness catching the breath.

Another Murmuration

They could be a plesiosaur,
                              now an upturned palm, scattering seed
– anything –
                    these few thousand starlings this dusk,
where the eye meets them   shoaling across the heavens,

at least in this hectare
                    and from this particular angle of the viewing platform.
They are forming, reforming with their next beautiful promise,
          lasting almost as long as the light.

Now they peel

down to roost in the reedbed
                                   as dark,
scrabbly, fidgety,
                    squabbling individuals
                                   with their own interpretations
and there they will have their separate sleeps.

Pity the poor warden and the volunteers in the reserve working party
after they've flown tomorrow, getting stuck into that cell of the habitat
    management plan;
all the bent-up reed, the bowed, claggy spikelets and such an ammoniacal stench.

The Pond
TG 34103 06385

Here's the start of a new sense of things –
just into March, the light and air fuller
and that mallard, so still there at the edge,
her heaviness pending, neck stretched,
not at rest; she can only be considering
her own streaked reflection, herself, held there
in the shade, and in the clay-backed mirror
of water, with no call for contact or confrontation,
just caught in a glance of the ways things are;
meeting a fresh slant of our mirrored selves;
now surely this is how it all begins, continues,
as this one, then another and then another.

Nest Surveying, II, 17/4/17
TL 87058 80969

This one's so well hidden –
grass, leaves and moss,
neat in a hollow
under dead vegetation.
Five robin chicks, parents off,
perfect for ringing.

We're exact with data –
grams on the digital scales,
then each individual's
crimped-on ring,
its letter and six numbers
we write into the science.

Now with the last but one
catching every nerve of my hands
with the hot throb and scratch
of pin feathers, and a faecal sac
clamminess, I'm caught.
The mother's back, bristling,

perched on the gorse,
at our head-height, no less
than four foot away.
Her whole desperation
fixed at my own gape. Fidgety
on my haunches

what am I midwife to?
Stood right in the face of this
ogrish outweighing of the odds,
she's singing autumn in spring –
displacing, though in no way wavering,
casting and re-casting ringlets of song.

Marbled Orb Weaver

This cling of stickiest silk
from the spirals of the web
and the tensile strength
of its signal thread –
that whole scheme set,
dew beading each node.
All her night work

now undone by my scythe
with one pass at the end
of this fresh-cut, rough acre ride
of four-foot-tall reed sweet-grass.
So she's here, in open fen,
her two centimetres scrambling
over the cuttings,

there's her egg-bloated
greeny-cream abdomen.
Look how she can't give in –
Jurassic proximity
of brain, venom gland, fang,
her book lung's unreadable
breathing; her palps,

each segment of forelegs
and the fused cephalothorax raised –
that fixed eye stratum
of a mountain unmoved
by any imposition, let alone
the chewed-raw-to-the-quick
of this fingertip.

Rides

After the brushcutters and rakes are away in the barn
and peat-clagged boots are kicked off by side or back doors
and all the rough clothes, sweated and smoked from the reed burn
are slung in their various heaps, and as all the lactic acid
settles through reaches of limbs that will ache now, the rest of this week

micro damages bed in, the length and breadth of each fresh-cut ride
where the job is never done and nothing rests in this long successional,
the cut-away remains only pended there by water;

so while the bath fills, steaming with muscle-soak and salts,
today the body and mind are one stubbled work,
the scrubby whole of it, this day justified in a salve of water.

Parasitoid and Host

Don't look for a point –
she's hinged now, arched
at the petiole, the little stalk
between thorax and abdomen
(details matter, it all matters
else nothing has or will)
so she's sprung, her nib already
darted its egg into that pulsing
fleshiness of swallowtail larva.

This ichneumon
finds them in the fen and only
pins them down for an instant.
Among these few Broad acres,
the umbels of milk parsley,
the fen-stink; don't think of it as spite
or care, but given and taken
infinitesimal materials
time and time and time again.

The larva will crawl on
to spin its tether and a fixed silk cap.
Then under that stuck cuticle,
through all the days to follow,
the altered chrysalis juices,
there's no denial or delay.
One will still come, though
not as first thought or intended,
something secreting;

a shifted emergence pattern
cut by hardened mouth-parts,
then a hauling-out, to stand
slicked, sure
in its wasp rigging,
dripping still
with the other, fully born
from the other, as we could never be
made so young or so fully formed.

The wood is too far a walk now
18/4/20

Whenever this lifts, it'll be long past
any chance of bluebells. All's to be done
is to think of them there, near their best
at that turn in the path amongst birches
where some new shade of the world is greening.

Though the mind unspools into their number –
more smoke-drift, apparition or shoal of blue.
The way a slim wildness insists in them
over the cool, wet earth and in each bowed head,
hung as an old man's, with a gasped heaviness.

Apocrypha I

That it was unlike anything other than this:
a herring gull's grey-white in the whiteness,
its pinkish feet paling on the lawn under snow.
Then all the sensitivity in the tip of a mole's snout
tump-breaching with a head of steam, bewildered,
out from its snug havoc of burrowing.

That the starved gull gagged it down alive
and still whole, then took to the air with a splitting cry
while the mole grappled the riddling oesophagus,
tore through the stomach wall and forced a way up,
out by the arch of the wishbone, but no further.
That it laid dead on the lawn, blood-black and smouldering.

First Nightingale

It can skulk, hide even, but you'll not get past
the end of this lane without hearing
its low–high phrases, one running into the other

now this, now this, this – leaving that cottage
on an edge of the fen. Thick scrub
both sides. But it's right-now-rightness, all-in

and impossible as the thought of an end
to desire. How can you sing, so full-bodied
to this coming night, this all-around tangle,

deep in amongst alder, elder, blackthorn,
bramble, hawthorn on the cusp and dog rose
and no doubt more and more dog rose?

I left before anything was said;
through dusk and that rough cover, so obviously
singing: in every part of me, singing.

Loke

Already the canopy's closed and the first flowers
have gone over, foxgloves are opening
with their fuller, lower lips and separate freckles
that draw me back in, to walk the same loke.

And through the insect-busyness of it all
that's still about the very last of the hawthorn,
that bramble bank and dog rose,
and the elder with each umbel so full of offers

I'm wondering how any of this ever works.
Despite everything, I'm thinking again
about our first wind-blown glances,

the grain and drift within each conversation
through so much fruit-set and blossom fall.
All those years and all our chances.

Wade's

Boredom spawns its own kinds of wickedness –
when we were kids, before they filled it in
for the bypass, we spent days and days

fishing there at the old gravel pit.
I remember Damian delivering
'the gummy': clutch set short,

bail arm down, he'd stand and full-toss cast
with any fresh-caught pissant roach or perch
still on the hook. We wouldn't even laugh,

but golf-clapped as just a jaw-part reeled back.
And Burrows, my best friend then, thirteen and furious
for only having caught gudgeon in droves,

tipped them from the keep-net, all parched
*O, O, O*s in the trampled grass while he boiled
the kettle on my little burner. That instant

he poured they stiffened, wide-eyed,
dotted like stuck exclamations. It's true
ignorance is bliss, and aren't we always told that

things come in threes? All our mothers dead
while we were still in our teens. Anyway, I'm sorry.
How you smiled, just now, triggered all this.

The Dreams of the Salmon Farmer and His Wife

I woke dead on the hour at twelve last night –
angel, you were running ripe, as if after a taste
of new water, thrashing in your sleep
how a hen fish cuts her redd, mouthing
and quivering towards a gape that wouldn't come.
There was nothing I could do to stir you.

Then in my own dreaming I was back
at the tanks in the hatchery, lifting out
fish after fish by the gills, fixing them
between arm and knee, and with my left hand,
pinching the length of the hens' then the cocks' bellies,
I was stripping all the roe and milt into a plastic bowl.

And in the mixing, I was lost again –
with my hand swirling a now bottomless swim
of so many thousand fathoms of eggs taking,
I was pulled in by the Atlantic jut of his kype,
all tatty, grizzled with an infestation of sea lice,
that drew away with our words and our wedding rings.

The Biology of Spiders

I want to unravel all the ways they work –
long past midnight, half-drunk with reading
and the no-sleep-potential of the last train,
for the ten minute walk from station to home
one word, *lumen*, hangs in my head.
It's right in the centre, like an orb weaver:
a strength of light or *inner, cellular space.*

And as I go the back way this small hour
suddenly there's her, squatting,
unsteady astride Give Way markings;
the minus-degrees squeeze on her bladder –
all legs, wonderful, embarrassed laughter
and a silken, amber flow decanted
down the gradient and camber of the side road.

Cat's Eye

You call me with the sadness of it,
roadkill on the path, *laid all wrong*,

and fretting whether the neighbours know.
It's gone by the time I'm home.

All except a small smear of blood
and this eye. It must have rolled clear,

or was left, being too much for whoever moved it.
The nerve-knot at the back is awfulness

but the eye is so much bigger, grander even,
a globe with an untouched gleam,

pure out of its orbit. Stilled
past all design and any slow affected blinking,

past all stalking or shitting the lawn;
immaculate, in fact. I'll hide it here

under the brightness of this lengthening day
with all the thrushes singing

and blue irises opening in our raised beds,
each of their petals velvety as a young cat's ear.

The Stag at the Gate

(after Ferenc Juhász)

It's time to bring the old boy home mother.
I've seen him, grubbing up crops, gnawing
at last year's cast antlers and everywhere stress behaviours –
fraying stands, and damage from browsing,
thinning all the life of the wood and hills.
Yes mother, I will bring your old boy home.

Zeroed, downwind, comfortable in my high seat,
stock-still and oh but I'm tired as a mountain.
How many head of deer have I taken?
He'll not look up here mother. In my tick-proof camouflage
I'm all the leaves of the wood-edge, and bracken,
green and at the turn – like his old tongue,

shape-shifted, flagging around, scenting hinds.
It is time. He's been belling for days now,
robed in mud from wallowing, and his pizzle
jerking out piss and muck, threshing the ground
with his old tines adorned with bramble. But that ruff
is thin, his craned neck too like a waning moon

and here he comes now, to the crossing tracks.
He's back to the gate. Oh I knew he would be.
He's such a poor old boy mother, on a bad knee, trying
to strip the gate post, rasping at snowy lichen from the top.
And I'm a cold mountain now. I am the most quiet now.
Mother did you hear the muzzle's bark?

Because it's done already, clean and down.
A good, true shot mother. In and through.
Here are all the stars coming out mother,
in the glaze of his eye. I'll be quick now
and as gentle about the gralloch, and all our faces
are there mother, in its fogged, shimmery glass

it's all hush and no rush. He's roped now with safe knots
and he drags so easily off the hillside mother, down
through the heather, back to the flatbed. And here he is,
so very soon, here he is, neck down and hoofless in the larder.
Oh mother, he'll not bolt again. Oh mother, here's his bag of pluck
with all the secrets of his wheezed lung and its last cry.

Hock

This is where the fields open, where it's no longer field but glazed
mud, pigs and their pens, slurried all the way to where the sun is
going in less than an hour or half hour and that glare is too much
through the carriage, this part of the line where it is just pigs, more
and more coming, snuffling, snouts, jowls, nipples, their great
mandibles grubbing, their trotters cloven in cold muck and of course
now there are crows, nothing's stupid, it's so cold there's one on a
sow's back, keeping its feet warm, how they behave, a colonnade of
hocks and all their pens arched as bomb shelters, the corrugated iron
shines uncanny and bright as the light washing out in here at this hour
bloodless and hinging as the old village butcher, Keeley,

ancient Keeley, cleavering hocks in his white coat, so white and ironed
with his pre-war hair, pomade and all his knowledge, studded later
with cloves they'd be blood oranges sizzling, so clean, that slicing
machine there, waiting at its passive angle, god, I never saw it working
but thought of it and I think of it now and the fizzing blue halo so
impossibly high up, I was just knee-high and that bulb blinking, the
insectocutor, with all the patience of the world.

Second-hand smoke

For whatever reason at the restructure meeting earlier
the HR person made reference to the October '87 storm,
I guess as a riddling way of saying *despite what you think*
you might know, always allow space for uncertainty.
Whilst someone whispered about smoke being blown up arses,
I sat there remembering that storm was the day of Grandad's funeral
and how Mum went uselessly bent double into that wind, trying
to cover her flowers in the short walk to the crematorium chapel,
but then I've nothing else. Though two days before, at the viewing,
the face of the younger man at the undertaker's who lifted the lid
is still crystal-clear. His tears at our tears landed on Mum somehow,
and as I think of it now, as an indelicate empathy maybe
and her hard-drawing on a fag when pissed off, the point of it
flaring, then a sharp exhale through tight-pursed lips. I still have
an occasional fondness for that trace on a stranger's clothes —
there was a woman, weeks ago, ahead of me in the queue
at the Co-op, about the age Mum should have been,
who ordered a pack of twenty, but not by the brand name,
she asked simply for *the ones with the diseased lungs.*
And the picture on that box of raw, restricted and blackened
off-symmetry reminded me of a red admiral I caught
playing outside Grandad's near the end while a boy about my age
whose face and name I can't recall, cupped his hands around it, or I did,
then genied the whole box of matches one or other of us stole
to light its wings, to see them blaze and just the small and vital ash of it.

Sedition Song

About every fallow stag's antler
cast in a stately acre, it runs out
with all the pheasant poults

through hedgerow, copse or field
and struts across A roads and B Roads,
crowing without any right of way

and it reports around the grouse butts
over all the moorland heather
where it drives the line of beaters

and that choking husbandry,
oh it burns the bog and the sphagnum moss,
spouts from larynxes knotted with tweed.

An Acte for the preservation of Grayne, 1566

The heads of any old Crowes, Choughs, Pyes, or Rookes, for the heades of every three of them one penny and for the heades of every six young Crowes, Choughs, Pyes or Rookes, one penny; and for everie six egges of them unbroken one penny: and likewise for every twelve Stares Heades one penny; for everie Head of Martyn Hawkes, Furskytte, Moldekytte, Busarde, Schagge, Carmarante, or Ryngtale, two pence; and for every two egges of them one penney; and for every Iron or Ospreyes Head Fower pence; for the Head of every Woodwall, Pye, Jaye, Raven, Kyte, one penney; for the Head of every Byrde which is called the Kings Fyssher; one peny; for the Head of every Bulfynche or other Byrde that devoureth the blowth of Fruite, one peny; for the Heades of everie Fox or Gray twelve pence; and for the Heades of every Fitchou, Polcatte, Wessel, Stote, Fayre bade or Wilde Catte, one peny; for the Heades of every Otter or Hedgehog, two pence and for the Heades of every three rattes or twelve Myse, one penney; for the Heades of everie Moldewarpe or Wante one halfpenney.

Chemical Chorus

DICHLORODIPHENYLTRICHLOROETHANE

ALDRIN   DIELDRIN   PARATHION   MALATHION

CHLORPYRIFOS   PHOSMET   AVERMECTINS

DICARBOXIMIDES   CLOTHIANIDIN

THIAMETHOXAM   FLUPYRADIFURONE

SULFOXAFLOR   IMIDACLOPRID   FIPRONIL

CHLOROTHALONIL   DICAMBA   METALDEHYDE

ALDICARB   PYRETHROIDS   CARBOFURAN

GLYPHOSATE   GLYPHOSATE   GLYPHOSATE

Ridge and Furrow

Here there's no soil sickness,
this old work's unimproved
under grass. Imagine
the yoked team of oxen,
a heavy-knuckled grip,
plough cutting, the mouldboard's
lift and turning over
each furrow to the right
and then the team turning
at the headland, stretching
the reversed S furlongs
rucking to the field top.
Team after team. After
the bone-sink push and plod
of each dead man and ox,
the gentlest earthwork now,
a balanced wet and dry –
Lady's smock and rushes
in the hollows; cowslip –
green-winged orchid, saw-wort
with meadow buttercup
and anthills on ridges
as far as the dew pond
up there at the rise end.

Tench

Stiff as a tongue with its nerve cut,
that tench surfaced, dead. From the clay bottom,
up past my untroubled night float,

it lapped with the dawn from the reed
to the pit's tapered end. I banked it.
The deepest green with blunt, black fins,

a slimy, muscled body, all rigored.
Full of the life that was and wasn't in it.
My child hands were slicked with the mucus

and while other fish were still out there rolling
there was no flinch or show of healing, just as here,
thirty years on there's nothing to be done

for the strongest men, dear to me, gone and going –
the something speaking then that laps again now
these dawns that can't be answered or thrown back.

Teneral

Forget the sounds, the changed breath
in his cheeks and neck, let each one go.
And the edge of that bed, the airflow mattress,
the shallow gasps of its cells transmuting

and forget the syringe drivers under the sheets,
interceding: let them go. And forget
those four December days, the bedside lamplight,
its faux stained-glass shade and dragonfly motif.

But think of the sun in May, a gentle day
for emergence; that there's an order
of things, even the waiting, somehow before

but after, holding his stilled hand, a similar chitin
in any moulted case, there past that form's pains
as all the atoms that flew together in him.

Earthstars

I don't have much truck with binomials
and anyway, this lot were first found at Cockley Cley,
so *Geastrum britannicum* just won't do for these
pre-Boudiccan shade-haunters. Look out for them –
fruiting provincials, dragging themselves into flesh,
staggering from this mud, their bodies still pushing
through all the Latinate, pine needle litter
with puffball heads round and dented as our vowels.

Apocrypha II

A hot mid-morning,
imagine the surprise for that day's congregation
when a stained-glass window shattered
and with that searing bolt of clear blue,
skidding past the altar, the rood screen,
onto the cold stone of the aisle between the pews,
was this bolus, about its rites: insect parts gorged
in the hinge of a swift's gape, itself pinned
by the clutch of a hobby, and that head-bowed
focus of its open, unyielding eyes.

Displays

I *Ophidiophobia*

There was too much encounter and presence in this case
so much so, in fact, we received vehement complaints.
Things had to go. First the obvious – the looped video
of what we assume are husband and wife in a roomful of cages,
that now itself seems a cage, the various species of snakes all idle
and someone else there, directing them, shadowy
at the back. Both he and she were smiling
as they rolled up their sleeves before pulling out
a puff adder. But of course, they then walked that rope of muscle
close to the camera for milking. Maybe it was that,
how she turned from its musk, how he latched the hinging jaw
to the lip of a fixed glass beaker covered with plastic
and thumbed the head there, as it cambered
on its fangs. It was as if they were fighting the force of a magnet.
Or maybe it was how the venom pooled out, all seminal.
On that first day the curatorial process became removal.
After the video, inevitably the Gaboon skull went,
with its slant, jagging whiteness, then the ebony wood carving
of unknown date, on loan from the anthropological museum
(traded – or stolen – some time from the Yoruba);
next was an actual empty beaker, prepped with unpierced plastic film.
But then even interpretation and captions were too much –
the comparisons of cytotoxic potency, the essential kinship
of venom to antidote, all of it just had to go
so in the end, behind the glass, we have only this
extendable stainless-steel snake hook.

II *Ornithophobia / Angelophobia*

Now this is the one I can't get past: a cuckoo specimen,
a female, displayed to show the developing egg
just there, off centre, waxing and white.
A dissected seraph somehow, with her grey wings resting –
though she's preened and ready, feet reaching, suspended
in this 18th-century jar, full to the brim with spirit.
It's the slant of that cut, made to take the head and breast –
the nick of each pared vertebrae and rib behind.
Then the potency and intent of that growth within,
right there, most beautiful and terrible and wanting,
back from when they would come and come to every parish,
renewing across the flyways, out of the oldest world. It has bisected
continents, our babel of hemispheres. That instinct from the egg
with a natal tooth and a hollow across each hatchling back;
the naked, blotched raw skin, with eyes closed as bruises,
in a head that can't balance but weighs and weighs again,
heaving out its own host on the cross of its shoulders.

Swallowtail

It came untouched through the wire,
down, along the trench, then was harried
like some raider on the sandbags of the fire step.

No more than a month from the first day,
up the line, near the Somme marshes,
as if life was suddenly in service to the beautiful –

so entire, with such colour and symmetry –
and not just the one with it cupped in his hands,
but all the others there, held waiting.

It was sent home in a Princess Mary Christmas tin,
the body relaxed on straw and wax paper.
And it's still there inside that new chrysalis, this same desire

we open and open again. The sun-bleached wings
more broken than imago, run through the ganglia
by what is and isn't a Mills bomb pin.

The germ of the world is one place

From all those bodies knocked to spots
or broken under the blitzed rubble
of their houses, out of that pulverised brick,
lime mortar, the flame and ash,

bursts of rosebay willowherb,
old-man-in-the-spring, Oxford ragwort,
thornapple, Thanet cress, off looting
each annexed margin for living space.

Spores

They'd daub the navel
of each newborn
with fulmar oil,

a cliff-nester's balm
easy to blame,
to latch on to

as the St Kildan midwives'
own infant lockjaw,
stored in gannet or sheep gut.

Either that or their blades,
unwashed and not first
passed through flame.

But what of all those before?
They rowed out, cutting
headlong into swells and gales

to open some westerly
ascetic distance,
some almost-disappearance

into a stink of fish and seafowl,
then lit beacons
from the highest point

just to say from among the breakers,
we are still here.
Whatever the life sought

there's no loneliness
for the spirit
in this husbandry,

under starlight,
on this ground
where that bacillus blooms.

Ballomania

What bugs me most isn't the plastic string
tied to the under-inflated balloon
or her game of *let-go-catch, let-go-catch,*
or her mum's *No!* as she keeps slipping her hand
in this tight space around the cases, full of trilobites,
ammonites and insects in amber
or that I'm hemmed-in with these strangers
and their stress at the base of the pedestal
when I just popped across on a whim at lunch,
wanting a look at the museum's great Irish elk,
it's impossibility of antlers displayed
with a fully-articulated skeleton.

It has something to do with the pink of her balloon,
how it's the same as her puffa jacket,
that it deepens to blood-vessely ripples
at the knot and now loosed, bobs its way in,
up from the pelvis like a bubble in some bone spirit level
all the way to the heart-end
and now she's on tiptoes, little aeronaut –
and it hits a sharp corner of a vertebrae and
oh, there's that secret bursting out of true
that I am still so unreasonably young to know.

Neurone

1/6/22

If anything might be immortal
let it be this – the first motor cell
sparking in a blackbird's head

in that moment, with the breath, before
lifting once more into song.
Here it comes again,

given to its territory. And now, again,
as I write this, in the current of listening –
it's a year to the dawn that we lost him.

All the attrition of those short months
of motor shutdown. His own speech gone,
re-wired through an *Eyegaze* and all the machines:

throat suction, CPAP, the hoist's whirring servo.
But each look, each desperate tenderness
kept on beyond exhaustion and urgent –

that last moment, among all those sparks
of blackbirds starting up in the dark, singing
where the least thing is to have given everything.

St Mark's Flies

I'd show you, if you let me,
come the hawthorn,
around some field or wood edge,

deep time hovering,
undiminished
by the name of any saint's day.

Their all-legs, slung-back
dangle, resolving in a strain
to nectar in that thick scent,

all that flower opening.
How a male settles to it –
head thick with what I want

to say is sagittal, that crest,
and the will of the mouth
feasting.

They are daemons fed-on-rot
in their fizzing cosmic black.
Familiars of the soil, they are

their own evangelists
bursting for the day and each
a clinker of our whole wild scenario.

Odonatologists' Anecdote

After all the flight seasons, mosquito bites,
sunburn, then winters, wading through papers,
working theories of dragonfly behaviours –
display, refusals, reproductions –
often just as glints in his mind's eye, then
chasing those reflections, wing strokes and shadows
down so many watercourses and flyways;

well, no field note was so ardent or true
as that one moment Hansruedi Wildermuth,
distinguished Swiss Odonatologist,
stood barefoot by his own garden pond
and along she came, tickling with a view
to oviposit in the thin shade of skin
just under the ball of his left ankle.

Amen

Grasmere Manuscripts

I

That prayer word, written again and again
throughout the drafting, fair copies, household sums,
recipes and the journaling, all the subtle changes
in the hand, grace notes in and around
the lines, testing – Dorothy's own word for settling
each new goose quill and this home-made ink:

II

an ounce of Gum arabick – 3oz Galls –
1oz sulphate of iron – a wine quart of water
of which put as much upon the Gum as will dissolve it
& the rest on the Galls & iron –
let it stand 3 days without cork – shake it –
after 3 days add the gum & it is fit for use

III

Out of my element but moved to think
even on a day like this, when the tops are cloud
and water, and their quicksilver veins off the fells
rise unstaunched as pools of liquid slate
in the near pasture, how that greylag grazing there
with one lifted feather – a left primary loosing, awry –
is kiltered now and clarified in its place
under this weather.

On the restoration of the cuckoo clock at Dove Cottage

From hill to hill it seems to pass,
At once far off, and near.

WILLIAM WORDSWORTH

It's priceless by association, all those blemishes –
cracks on the face, corrosion and dust
clogging the innards, the spindle and gears.

Tending a broken thing back requires close pains,
watching it move, to see where it lags or shifts,
then the vision for making it real.

Yet returned to his cottage, on the turn of the stairs,
there's still bad torque on that pendulum, a new weight
on the hands and it's calling all wrong measures

too late to the growing, in and around the cottage garden –
all that's quickening (leaf burst, the flush of caterpillars,
the weave of dunnock, reed warbler and pipit nests).

No first letter will be sent to *The Times*
from any near parish, now there's no bird calling
its own name, here, at this northern end of the one flyway.

Horse chestnut

In rude health, almost obscene –
this full leaf, wet-look, already lit
with hundreds of candles, spikes
of pinkish white flower, all bursting
from a yellowy basal blaze –
it's only early May
but this unstressed spread and shade
forsakes nothing at the roadside,
standing trunk-centred through swirls –
the wind in heat, hankering
for gusts of rain, for nut-heaviness,
to bleed canker and know leaf scars.

Apocrypha III

There's something hell-bent in such desire –
that a wet winter and spring over-topped banks
and brought a pike to this: a body bend, bursting up
to the rays of its fins, snapping sideways
say, after a coot or moorhen. Snagged itself here,
the heavy belly forked on its own thick folds
in the gnarls of a sallow.
                                        Now in a shock of heat,
under blackened eyes, in its putrefying gawp,
the miraculous: dry grass woven around
conical incisors, a cup of mud and moss
in that bowl of pike-mouth, lolling,
so that the right gill plate visors this too-much-sun
for the five blackbird chicks, near to fledging,
each straining to out beg the other.

On the snail in medieval manuscripts

They proliferate, crowding
in margins, somehow
to do with resurrection,
coming out of one's shell,
or the fight against sloth.
So a visored knight
on his best horse goes full tilt
to lance one horned beast
at the far-end of a leaf stem,
curling the edge of the text.
Though God knows what hell
is going on with the hare
astride a smiling lurcher,
riding out for the hunt
with a snail tethered
to his hawking gauntlet.
Then there's this scene,
decidedly unilluminated
relating to a poem
with no clear outcome:
two men-at-arms
with their broad swords
and a woman in between
in an aspect of protestation
at the huge one on the rampart
of a homely castle,
its antagonistic muscle
raised and lengthened, proud
of its shell and rendered
inquisitive with such exquisite
detailing of the vulvic
and sac-skin wrinkliness
of its foot, draping
the battlements' teeth.

Courtship

I'm thinking here of that woodlouse spider,
the pure oxygen, blood-red arcing of legs,
the abdomen akin to a sheep tick, engorged,
still thirsting after a long drink. But more than that

those armoured, fulsome mouth-parts – the chelicerae.
Kuh-lis-*uh*-ree – say it with me, like a sweet nothing,
a shibboleth. Gaped. All the risk and need
of the tussle, this hinge to brace and bite against.

We all have needs

Take these, just two days back and hawking –
swifts, yielding such screams
low now after a storm over freshwater,
pressure unbroken, heat pooling, all nerves
running the length, each notch of vertebrae –
and their dashed couplings, drawing each body,
every call, each scream-chasing contact
to the re-entry smoulder of themselves.

All the more risk in the second thirst,
this next descent, level and lift –
mouth open, fathoming the right angle
to drink only at a skim, a slam of cold
that could douse the back of the throat
and down the head under these heavy shoulders.

Purple

In this latest heat,
the throb and drag
too-much-of-it,
amongst that weight,
the will and sheer fall
of these longest days;
even now, though unseen,
there are certain
and sayable things:
there's still groundwater,
at least enough
for the roots of this oak –
and there'll be aphids
and the moving through them
of a glut of honeydew
(more than once
considered manna) and
that there's more than one way,
one time. Here
are versions emerging,
these glimpses, these
folded silhouettes,
of purple hairstreaks,
we've only the imagined
wing-phasing between
under and upper –
in this one year,
this high summer
the whole of that life
without any need
to flit down from the top
of the oak's canopy.

Reedbed in August

Let's slip off this path, keep the Yare at our backs,
go far past the end of the last-cut ride,
more than the acre in, that's well out of hearing.
The reed will screen us to a higher horizon –
its push of organelles, green stems,
purplish blooms, all loose and silky with growing.

Let's turn right into that wildness,
for now is only this hot press of a storm to break –
and while that sky may well be full of grief
and here's as broad as it can ever be,
just look how the reed rushes to it. Here
there is good hunkering for the moulting.

Trespass Song

Old as the heath but this new taste of it darling,
past desire path, bridleway, heath-burn and firebreak
darling, all the singing territories,
jagging the fence line, the gorse-spiked border, heather
and browned bracken stands, darling, their unfurled fiddleheads
and over salt-licks, lichen, moss, spores and sporing darling,
along the barbs of the wire belling through a headwind
darling, and each unvelveted tine. And all this saltiness

thickens, my love, with the red stag's tongue
and the scratched-after itch, my love, in its shaggy flanks
is a wallowed mire of ticks, my love, still bristling

there at the wire, my love, and in these knots of scut
my love, with coarse, unspinnable snuff, my love,
all the grace notes darling, so come snag them with a leap.

Familiars

Wiping sweat from both temples with my wrists
on first waking today, returned me to the work
of this: those years ago, and somewhere
between dream and memory, grafting

at Blackwater Carr with loppers and bow saw,
processing felled sallow. My back still bent
from the task and blind-sided. Then the sense
of another life drawn close and watching,

no more than an arm's length from behind the reed-fringe,
with all the simple and compound eyes
of day moths, orb weavers, late dragonflies
and whatever-flies; a mammal weight,

an almost-known scent and their soft tread closing.
Their close, curious mind working, as mine is
first felt in the hind of the chest, then
the caught mid-breath quick of it; a moment

meeting some readiness, some shade
of love, of grief, moving at the shoulder.
My small repair of listening but saying nothing
this time, of keeping on and not turning.

Sedge Warbler

TG 33863 06105

Think of it Darling, that busy voice in the reed
now back in our patch. So confiding,
how it came closer, rendering versions
of what I can only call its rhapsody.

The mimicry in amongst its own notes –
buzzard, magpie, blue tit, tern,
flight calls of linnet, even greenshank.
His whole craning, throat-puffed effort.

The perfect pitch of a true listener.
He'll be dusk-singing now, threading phrases
from that bed. The length of the night-flown
flyway, up from sub-Sahara,

Iberia to here, across great deltas
of language, Niger-Congo, Romance;
via constellations; Gondwana; hydrogen;
the cosmic web condensed in his head.

Where four-spotted chasers make a window in the fen

Look eastwards, you'll be better off on your knees to see
dragonflies, dew burning off them, and the reed,
and the mist from the pool's near bank – freshwater
warming, brighter now, golden, green-golden, even.

And then there's this gathered clan of chasers,
their braced panes blazing, each back-lit node and vein
roosting, in torpor, still settled from the night.
And in this sunk galaxy they've made a reedlight

of their wings. Look at each stemmed body,
each staunch little clasp. Look again now
at that highest one, fully set in this dawn sun

stirring the globes of his eyes – see each facet's gleam.
Of all that can be or might be done, tell me again.
From here, you know, I'd believe almost anything.

Exuviae Survey

TG 33974 06301

Here's one, low on a stem of saw sedge,
see how the dyke's now in favourable condition –
water soldier, frogbit, good airy water.
And all this at the edge, there for the nymph

to crawl up and cling to at their last
ministering before emerging. Note it here,
a kind of loss, moved on from,
the time given and all groundwork done.

I don't tend to the Latin names, I know this
as the whole case of a Norfolk hawker –
the waferish, moulted thing, standing-to,
earthed, to be kindled under the tongue.

Nettle-tap

Come with me, now that May
has gone from the hedges
and this season of weddings is past,
flitted into fine moth-hours
of such short, humid nights.

I'll show you two day-flyers,
settled in the cool of a nettle patch,
big and nicked as the nail on your ring finger;
duskier confetti; unfolded notes for robin song,
in cop, each the other's half of one diamond.

Though the singing season's done with

here's what I most want to remember:
right now, the heat on a day like this,
every window and the side door open,
the air thickened and full of the bundling
cottony-white of black poplar seeds.
See how they spin and drift. Gathering first
in the corner of the back room, the kitchen –
really, they're a bloody mess, cushioning
the carpet on every tread of the stairs.
May they always. This evening and tonight
Darling there's no need to fuss or clear it,
let's sleep with the windows wider
as all our years, those before and to come,
let's wake to its mantling everywhere.